Osvaldo Golijov

Tekyah

for Chamber Ensemble

Full Score

Archive Edition

HENDON MUSIC

BOOSEY & HAWKES

AN IMAGEM COMPANY

DISTRIBUTED BY

HAL•LEONARD® CORPORATION
7777 W. BLUEMOUND RD. P.O. BOX 13819 MILWAUKEE, WI 53213

www.boosey.com
www.halleonard.com

Published by Hendon Music, Inc.
a Boosey & Hawkes company
229 West 28th Street, 11th Floor
New York NY 10001

www.boosey.com

 AN IMAGEM COMPANY

ISMN 979-0-051-09727-2

First printed 2004
Second printing 2009

*Written for the BBC Music Film
commemorating the 60th anniversary of the liberation of Auschwitz*

Instrumentation

Clarinet in B♭
Accordion
3 Horns in F (all doubling Shofar)
3 Trumpets in B♭ (all doubling Shofar)
2 Trombones (all doubling Shofar)
4 Shofars

Notes

Accordion: all glissandi are to be played with an electronic pedal

Clarinet: + and ₒ indicate to use alternate fingerings for the same pitch

      "davenen" means to imitate the traditional chanting used for private Jewish prayers

      indicates a Klezmer gracenote or "kvetch"

Shofars: the shofar players should play the traditional Jewish shofar calls (Tekyah, Shevarim, Truah, and Tekyah G'dolah) where indicated. Measure 30 indicates how these calls are played (if the player is unfamiliar with them). After that they are not written out, but should be played in the same manner. Note that the actual pitches may be different depending on the individual shofars used; this is perfectly acceptable.

∧   indicates a long fermata

duration: ca. 6 minutes

Written for the BBC Music Film commemorating the 60th anniversary of the liberation of Auschwitz

TEKYAH

Osvaldo Golijov

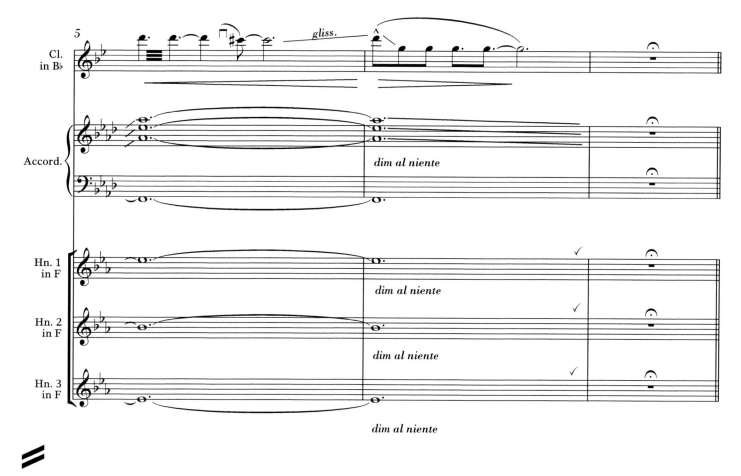

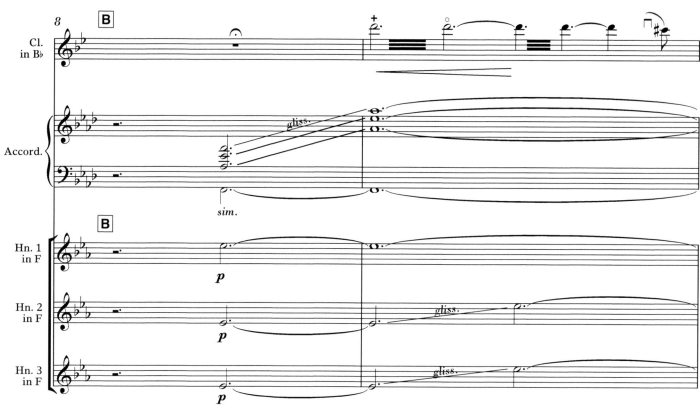

4

10

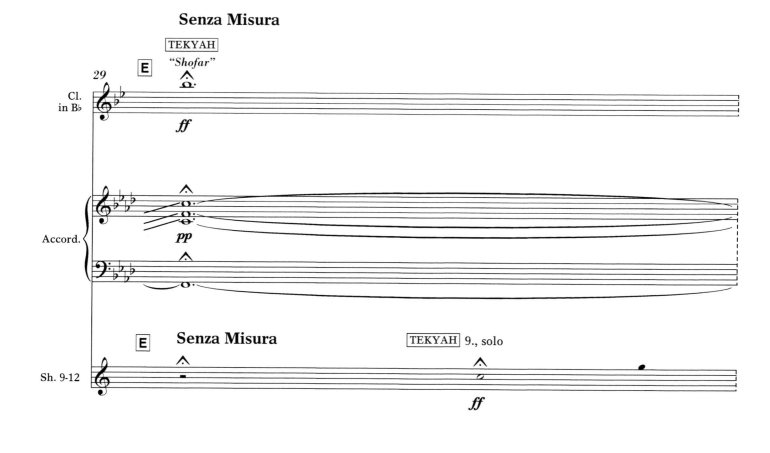

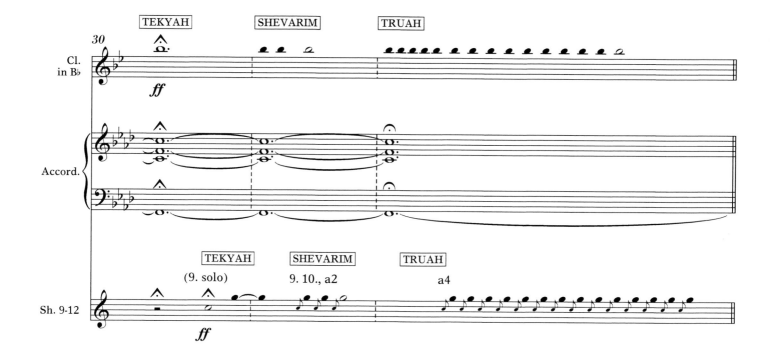

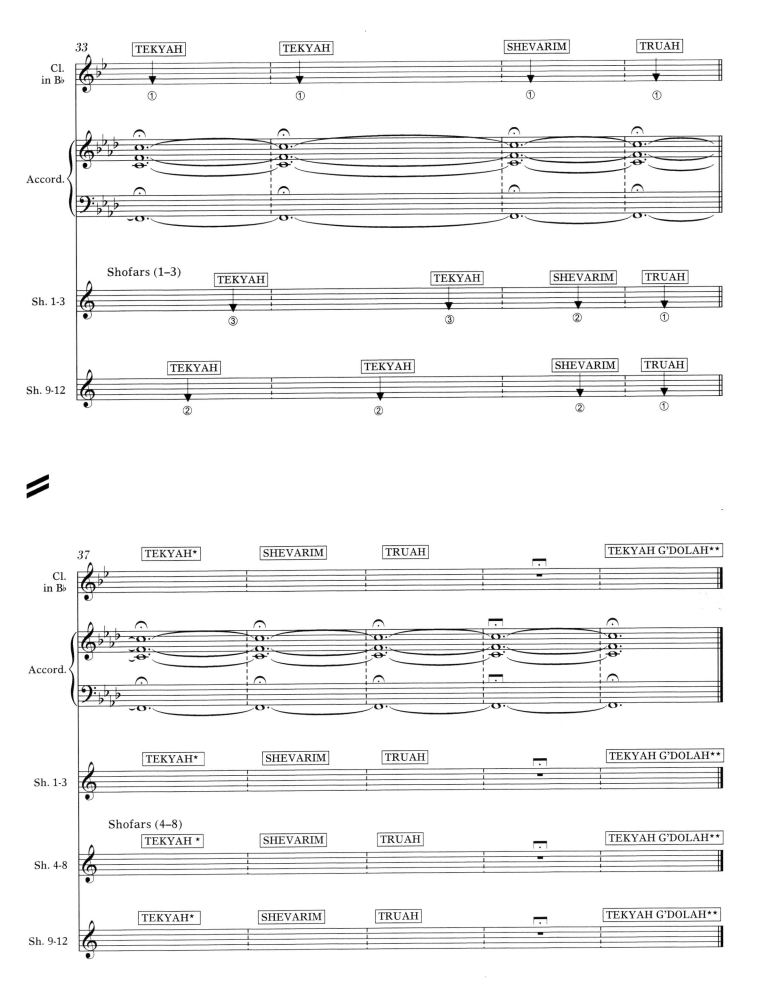

* Each player starts independently after every bar.
** As long as possible (independent lengths).